Fit through love

Fall in love with fitness, yourself, and your life!

By Adrienne Rivera

MEET THE AUTHOR

ADRIENNE RIVERA

Adrienne Rivera is a fitness coach specializing in helping you creating transformational, healthy lifestyles in all areas of life. She believes that long term physical & emotional health can only come from mastering relationships with others, food, fitness, and most importantly oneself.

Adrienne is also a motivation speaker, triathlete, and host of the podcast, "The Fit Through Love Show." She is a National Academy of Sports Medicine Certified Personal Trainer and has a degree in Psychology. She has worked with clients to help them lose up to 50 pounds, helped couples mend their relationships, and assisted many in fixing their relationship with food.

Find her at **adriennerivera.com**, on Instagram at **@fitthroughlove**, or on Facebook as Adrienne Rivera.

To learn more about her about coaching, speaking rates, and retreats send her an email her at **adrienne@adriennerivera.com**!

PRAISE FOR *FIT THROUGH LOVE*

"Adrienne Rivera's wisdom and unique perspective of working on your relationship with fitness and bringing more love into your life has really expanded my perspective. The guidance that you're about to receive here in Fit Through Love has the ability to improve your relationships with yourself and others. Through Adrienne's wisdom, I have seen dramatic growth in my relationships and I've created more self-love. Simply by creating more love in my life, my business has grown, I've started to prioritize myself and, as Adrienne puts it in this book, I am now operating from an abundance mindset."

"I was really surprised at the angle that this book took. It offered such a holistic approach to life and how we get to include fitness as a tool to positively impact all of the other areas of our life. Most self-help books exclude fitness, and most fitness books only talk about the how-to's of fitness. It was refreshing to begin to look at fitness through the lens that this book does—through your relationship with it. I learned that once I start to look at areas of my life such as relationships, money, fitness, food, and spirituality through a relational lens, I can see how all things are interwoven and impact each other. I am motivated to really take my fitness to the next level to see how it begins to take everything else in my life up a notch."

CASEY NICOLE FOX
author of I Quit: How to Quit on The Things That Are Holding You Back in Life Instead of Yourself

"Fit Through Love truly offers a unique perspective on how to get into the healthiest version of yourself. I loved that it wasn't all just about fitness—the key components about mindset, relationships, and communication offered a lot of value to helping me become healthy from a mental and emotional level as well."

Mette Glargaard
author of How to handle the classic narcissist - in families, in relationships, and in the workplace

"This is a fantastic read for anyone who is looking to improve their health and life. It's an inspiring and refreshing point of view."

JAMIE HERNANDEZ, M.A.
author of Eat the Berries, Weight Loss for Busy Moms

"This book gave me clarity on what I wanted and how to get it. Great read!"

PETRA RAKEBRANDT
author of YIN IS THE NEW BLACK- How to get ride of imbalances in life

"An outside-the-box view on health and fitness—focusing on the true motivation for positive change, mindset and LOVE."

KRISTEN ZANONI
author of Focused and Fancy

"For a long time, I didn't take much time for myself.

It wasn't until I made a conscious decision to start working on myself did I realize how important I still am. Adrienne helped me find a way to deal with my stress and personal issues in a positive way. With Adrienne's help, I have been improving my body & mindset and it's noticeable to everyone. Every day my body wakes up happy and I'm so excited about life. I am so grateful to have her as my coach and can't wait to see what the next 3 months bring."

MELISSA, V
Online fitness + mindset coaching client

"One of the most powerful books for health, fitness, relationships, and self-love you will read. Adrienne's knowledge and story will empower millions of people including you."

ARMANDO AGUILAR
CEO of Live Big CEO

"Fit Through Love guides you through your own path to fitness, happiness, and success. Adrienne Rivera is a light and a source of energy for achieving your dreams by mastering your overall mindset."

TRAVIS GREENLEE
Best selling author of Living Your Life on Purpose in the Real World

Fit through love

Fall in love with fitness, yourself, and your life!

By Adrienne Rivera

Dedicated to the love of my life, Darren.
For filling me with love every single day
For believing in me and supporting me every step of
the way—especially during the challenging times.

Thank you for being the example of how life is made
up of relationships
Thank you for motivating and inspiring me to have
a healthy relationship with food, fitness, others, and
most importantly myself.

Everyone is worthy of having a life of love, laughter,
health, fun, and adventure
Darren, you remind me of that every single day.

AND IT ALL STARTS WHEN WE LEARN TO LOVE
OURSELVES

FIT THROUGH LOVE AT A GLANCE

INTRODUCTION + MY STORY   1

VISION: WHAT DO YOU WANT IN LIFE?   13

BUILD YOUR FOUNDATION WITH COMMUNICATION   32

CREATING HEALTHY RELATIONSHIPS   44

YOUR RELATIONSHIP WITH FITNESS   54

LEARNING TO LOVE YOURSELF   63

BUILDING A HEALTHY RELATIONSHIP WITH FOOD   75

MASTERING MINDSET + MOTIVATION: INTEGRATION   90

INTRODUCTION + MY STORY

"It takes courage...to endure the sharp pains of self discovery rather than choose to take the dull pain of unconsciousness that would last the rest of our lives."

- Marianne Williamson

YOUR GREATEST "WEAKNESS" IS ACTUALLY YOUR GREATEST STRENGTH

TAKE A DEEP BREATH IN.

You are WORTHY of the life that you want. You are worthy of LOVE! You are love. You are LOVE. YOU ARE LOVE! As you breathe out, tell yourself, "I am love." Beautiful. Now wrap your arms around yourself, SQUEEZE yourself tight. How does it feel? How does it feel to love yourself? When was the last time that you hugged yourself?

What has been in the way of you allowing yourself to love yourself more? The meaning of life is love. Your journey into self-love has begun. Prepare yourself to up-level all relationships in your life.

Life is all about relationships. You may be thinking this book is all about romantic relationships… and while you'll definitely be learning about the significance of romantic relationships, the purpose of this book is to step back and look at life through the lens of all relationships. I'm talking about your relationships with food, alcohol, fitness, yourself, and everyone in your life!

Our perspectives in life can both heal us and destroy us. Throughout this book, I ask for you to allow me to guide you into having the perspective of life through the lens of relationships.

MY STORY OF LEARNING HOW TO LOVE MYSELF

I had lost all control. I had lost hope. I tip-toed down the stairs of my parents' house down into the kitchen to eat my stress away... to find love through food. It was late at night after I had already gone out to eat with my family at a Chinese restaurant. I had polished my plate, I was full. Yet I felt like I had no control over the pre-portioned meal. I needed to go eat more. I needed to do it in secret.

"What if my mom wakes up and hears me rummaging through the pantry?" I thought. I was afraid that I was going to upset her or to make her mad. I had already eaten a huge meal! What was wrong with me?

And yet at the same time, I was loving this secret that I was harvesting that was only mine. I protected this secret. I later on learned how much my binge eating disorder was thriving in secrecy.

We always want what we can't have.

We seek thrill, adventure, and risk. This is dangerous. I was in denial about having a problem. I didn't want to admit it to others or be present to the fact that I was using food for comfort and to release stress.

One day I was driving to the gym when my car seemed to make the decision for me to stop at Wegman's first. I bought a 6 pack of Strawberry Yogurt and protein bars and drove to the gym parking lot. Thoughts of anxiety and perfection attached to the workout I was about to do kept me cemented in my seat. I thought to myself, "I'll just have one yogurt before I work out so that I have enough energy to go all out." Before I knew it, I entered a mental void where my mind went blank and I inhaled ALL of the yogurts in the gym parking lot.

The evil, familiar, fake-comforting voice came back into my head saying, "it's okay, just have another." The act of food and eating gave me comfort—which was something that I felt like I didn't have in my life at the time. I wanted to avoid my workout, avoid pain and discomfort. I wanted to hide.

Several years passed and I walked out of Owen's dining hall at the Virginia Tech college campus after eating, full of stress and avoidance for all of the work that I had to do. Then I walked to 2 more dining halls in a row right after that. I was running away from my fears and being controlled by my thoughts and by the act of eating food.

It wasn't until winter break after my freshman year of college that I really knew that I had a problem and I needed to go get support. I felt hopeless and embarrassed. I was hiding snacks in my dresser, I didn't know how to ask for help. I knew that my mom was the one that would help me break free of this cycle. I also knew that if I started talking about it, I would cry.

I pulled out my laptop and proceeded to write a 5 page detailed essay for my mom to read about what I was dealing with and how she could help me.

Luckily, she was so understanding. Her only wish was for me to have asked for help sooner. She got me to go to a counselor at college. When I got to my first appointment with my counselor, I was shaking in fear. Speaking it out loud was the scariest thing that I could've imagined doing—because hearing myself say it out loud this time made it true. I hated admitting what I was dealing with.

It was as if the evil comforting voice that I would hear in my head during binge eating episodes came back to haunt me, pounding its fists on the walls of my brain like someone trapped in a dark room. It was safe in my head, but as soon as I started to speak about what I was dealing with, it became a story instead of something that was inside of me.

The more and more comfortable I became sharing my story, the more it became just that—a story

It was no longer what I thought was simply who I was,

it was just a story. It lost more and more power over me the more I talked about it—until eventually, I forgot what it was like to hear that voice in my head.

I became free. I embraced that voice and offered it compassion for providing me with the comfort that I was needing at the time. The voice finally vanished once and for all because it no longer served me. And it feels amazing to have said goodbye to that voice that lived inside my head and to be present enough with myself so that I can tune in and allow it to be nourished and full after every meal.

Would you believe me if I told you that I struggle to find motivation to wake up early in the morning and work out?

When I first moved to Steamboat after graduating from Virginia Tech, I didn't have a job for the first 2 months that I was there. I fell into a "funk" where I was sleeping in until noon, making cheese bread (toast with melted cheese, WHY DID I DO THAT!), and then telling myself that I would work out at some point because I had "ALL DAY" to do so.

...And guess what, it didn't happen! The problem was that I had ZERO accountability and I wasn't clear on my end goal or what I really wanted to do!

I decided that I deserved to do what I loved, motivating others to find a healthy lifestyle. I wanted to be an online fitness coach!

So what did I do?

I listened to podcasts for months, I researched for months, I TRIED DESPERATELY to download all of the free business building resources I could find and you know what happened? Absolutely nothing.

I was learning so much but I was OVERWHELMED with all of the information. And I had no clue on earth where or how to start!

I was wasting my time and I wondered if I should just give up! Maybe starting the business of my dreams just wasn't for me.... I started to think, "maybe I'm just not good enough, or smart enough.".

MY OLD NEGATIVE SELF TALK PATTERNS WERE COMING BACK!

I thought my mindset was the only problem. So I bought an $1,000 12-week program to help my mindset. Wanna know what happened?
I had better beliefs, thoughts, and I was motivated. BUT... I still wasn't doing anything for my business. I

was scared at the thought of putting myself out there on social media. I didn't know where to start. And I was scared of being vulnerable.

So then I saved up, spent all of my savings, and hired a business coach who only works with Online Fitness Coaches and teaches them how to build their businesses for $5,000.

Want to know what happened?

I STARTED MY BUSINESS AND STARTED CHANGING PEOPLE'S LIVES!!!

I was financially held responsible and I was in an amazing support group with other online fitness coaches that were setting themselves up for success!!!

Now, let me just be clear for a second. I didn't have "an extra $5,000" just laying around. That was ALL OF MY MONEY but I knew that I needed to invest in myself at a level that scared me enough to actually DO IT.

It was the best decision I ever made! With that program I also got weekly mindset coaching calls for myself, and my life changed! How could I fully commit 1,000% of myself to the SUCCESS of my clients if I wasn't investing in myself? Simple, I wouldn't have been able to.

Now I use the coaching, education, and resources that I've gotten for myself to then make sure that my clients won't fail.

90% of people give up on what they start...
You won't give up...
I WON'T LET YOU....

I am rooting for your success and I won't stop until you break free from what's holding you back!!!

Pause real quick. If you can't tell - my overarching goal here is to: Help you AVOID falling in the same holes I did during my journey to finding mental freedom and building a healthy relationship with food...

Over the years, I tried all of the "diets." I was vegan for half of a summer... I was paleo for a few months (which I did feel amazing with, but found that it was too restrictive for myself... I tried the cabbage soup diet, the south beach diet, and the abs diet with my mom...

And years later, I found out that RESTRICTING myself was the problem after all and it gave me so much anxiety! Even tracking my calories made me freak out and feel restricted. Dieting wasn't right for my body, wasn't right for my goals, wasn't safe at all, and actually didn't even work! - but hey, you don't know until you KNOW, right?

So, in case you try what has worked for me, meal

prepping... I've got a free "Meal Prep Starter Kit" to help you start meal prepping and make it SUPER EASY to always have yummy, healthy food ready for whenever you need it... email **adrienne@adriennerivera.com** if you want it!

Now, back to my story! I invested in myself! And I would never go back! I couldn't picture myself not having a mindset coach now. It's been so crucial in my life and my breakthroughs.

My vision for you is to live a fit life full of love—both self love, and endless love from the people around you.

You are worthy of the life you want to live simply because you were born! I'm on a mission to transform the mindsets of as many people as I can so that everyone knows and feels WORTHY of their biggest dreams. So let's discover YOUR vision and dive right in!

EXERCISE: Do you journal? I recommend 5 minutes of journaling a day! Throughout this book, you will see different exercises for you to do at the end of each chapter. The exercise that I invite you to do in this chapter is journal about what health and wellness means and looks like to you. Write about how you currently feel and how you want to feel. Write about why your mental and physical health are so important to you.

VISION: WHAT DO YOU WANT IN LIFE?

"Nobody—not a voice of authority, not your mama, not the foremost expert in your arena—gets to tell you how big your dreams can be. They can talk all they want but you get to decide if you're willing to listen."

- Rachel Hollis

WITHOUT
VISION,
WHERE WILL
YOU KNOW
WHERE
YOU'RE
GOING?

I want you to FANTASIZE.

What do you want in life? What do you really *really* want? I'm talking about dreaming big—no limitations, no rules, no financial constraints... What would you paint on the canvas that is your life?

What's coming up for you when I ask that question? It's such a simple question, yet it can be hard to answer. A myriad of situations probably come to mind, swirling around without any clarity to them.

One reason it's so hard to answer is self-doubt, the inability to dream BIG because of a feeling that your ideal life isn't for you, that you don't deserve what you desire. When daydreaming about your perfect life, your brain dismisses this idea of perfection as a complete fantasy, thinking it's so far away from those goals that they become impossible. You come up with excuses, reasoning that you just weren't made to have the life you've always wanted, that other people are just more special than you or had a head start in life.

STOP CREATING STORIES THAT NO LONGER SERVE YOU.

We are meaning-making creatures that rationalize everything in the form of creating justification "stories."

Example: When you don't get the job that you want, the story you create is that you aren't qualified or smart enough for the job.

Universe: "Actually, I have something way better in store for you."

Example: When you slip up on a diet and gain the weight you've been trying to shed, the story that you make up is that you just don't have the willpower to have the body of your dreams.

Universe: "Actually, I'm throwing you opportunities and challenges that you can actually use to strengthen your willpower."

See, here's the thing: Everybody, including you, has the freedom to break away from limitations and be the designer of their life.

Everybody has a different vision. Everybody has different goals. My task for you in this first chapter is to find yours, to picture what you want and to picture it *without* influence from others.

One reason that you find yourself lost in life is because you took a path that somebody else laid down for you, following it blindly into the forest until one day you stop, look around, and realize that you should have brought YOUR OWN compass. Instead of dejectedly putting your head down and traipsing ahead on the wide, comfortable path going the wrong way, you could do things differently...

You could take out a map and see all the less traveled options out there. All of the majestic mountains and pristine lakes that can be accessed simply by just listening to yourself.

Sure, there may be some river crossings, some deep canyons, some steep slopes filled with loose sand, but how would it feel knowing that you're tackling these obstacles with a full heart, knowing that they're leading to a place you never thought you could get to? And once you've gotten over them, how would it feel to look back over what you've just crossed and realize that you're fulfilled and truly happy?

YOU GET TO HAVE ALL OF THE THINGS THAT MAKE YOU HAPPY.

Before conquering all these obstacles, it is imperative that you look onto the map and figure out exactly where you want to be. It could be that you're right next to where you want to be. It could be that you're a million miles away. I want you to realize that you can make it there, that people can help you along the way and that you're not alone. The first step is to dissolve the doubts in your head that push you in the wrong direction and block you from realizing your goals.

THE FIRST STEP IS YOU HAVING BELIEF IN YOURSELF!

STOP FOR A SECOND

Stop. Look at yourself. REALLY STOP. Look at yourself in their mirror. Block out the negativity and excuses swirling around you. Where, in your heart, do you want to be? What gives you goosebumps? What do you spend your days daydreaming about while you're doing something you're not passionate about? What makes you feel good about yourself? What do you wish you could do more of? Who are you? Who do you want to be? What do you love doing?

Your answer will come easy to you, because you've always *known* what you want. You've just been afraid to find it because of perceived judgments from others and EXCUSES that block your wildest dreams.

Invite your new idea of yourself in and focus on it. Picture every single aspect of what makes this idea perfect for you. And the reason it's perfect for you is because you are being you. The deepest, most stripped down version of you. That version of you, the true you without any guards up, knows exactly what it wants. It has always known what it wants, and it can have it. That version of you is not afraid.

So here we go. Buckle your seatbelt! Because that version of you is a on a mission to live the life that you know was meant for you, without settling. Focus on that dream, that goosebump-inducing passion that you want to make into reality. It's very likely that you've had your vision in the back of your head this whole time, halfheartedly pursuing it while straying from it in another direction. Maybe you want to start traveling the world as a digital nomad. Maybe you want to start a new business. Whatever it is, it has always been an idea inside of you that you've wanted to do but just... haven't.

THE PUZZLE

One reason I find that people are hesitant to pursue the trail that's right for them is because they don't know what it looks like for them. They are hung up on which puzzle pieces need to be put together to make that final picture. So to visualize your dream, first do some research. Ask for help. Break it down and find out what pieces are part of your final picture.

Most likely, these pieces all boil down to one thing: Relationships.

Life is made out of *relationships*. I'm talking about your relationship with the following: fitness, food, alcohol, your significant other, your friends and community, your parents, your coworkers, your pets, your garden, and money. These are all relationships. And all relationships get to be *intentional*, full of love and compassion.

In your vision, you want to be physically fit enough to feel amazing and be in shape to say 'YES' to anything that you want to do. You want a partner that supports you and lifts you up, you want friends that see the true you and want to see you happy and fulfilled. You want to realize that your parents are proud of you because you're happy and you're doing something meaningful to you. You want coworkers that are working with you to create a common vision. You want your pets to be taken care of and your garden to be healthy and vibrant as a result of the energy you've poured into it. You want money to be an asset and a motivation for pursuing this vision, not a crutch and a reason to stop you. You want your living space to be full of good energy and a place to bring together people and ideas.

Nobody creates a negative vision for themselves. Nobody pictures themselves in their dreams as being abused and torn down, dependent on others, broke and lost. The sad reality is that many people are lost just because they haven't paused and looked at themselves to determine what they actually want out of life. Of course you don't want to create a negative vision for yourself. You don't want to picture yourself as having low self-worth.

A combination of every single second of your life has gotten you to be somewhere special, it's where you are now. You get to ask yourself what has happened in your life to have led you to the current mindset and relationship you have with certain things in life.

Sometimes, we need to ask for help. From spirit, a friend, a book, and/or a coach. And if you're reading this book & want help finding clarity on your vision, go to **adriennerivera.com** and schedule a time to speak with me or someone on my team. I'm here for you and I'm so excited for you to start living your vision!

WHAT DOES YOUR VISION FOR YOUR LIFE LOOK LIKE WHEN YOU PAUSE & LOOK WITHIN?

FINDING YOUR WHY

Goal setting is one of the most popular things to do in today's society. DREAM BIG! Dream it into reality! Hooray! I love the optimism. But, what is the missing link when it comes to why so many people don't actually follow through on their goals? Why do so many people that set New Years Resolutions quit on working towards those goals before February?

The answer? Because their goals aren't SPECIFIC! And they fail to create an action plan. Perhaps you've heard of the acronym "SMART" goals. Well, many articles are now raving about the revision to "SMARTER" goals. And the "ER" makes all of the difference!

S = Specific
M = Measurable
A = Achievable
R = Relevant
T = Time-bound
E = Evaluated
R = Recognized/Rewarded

Let's apply this to an example. Let's chose the most common New Year's resolution— "I want to lose weight."

The reason why this goal is isn't the best is because it fails at the first level of the acronym! How much weight?

Revised goal: "I want to lose 50 lbs"

Perfect! Now the goal is more specific and it is measurable. Is the goal achievable? If you have 50 pounds to lose then yes, it probably is achievable. But, maybe you only need to lose 10-20 lbs! So many people get stuck on a certain goal weight that they had many years ago. If they tried to get back to a weight they had in high school, it would not be healthy.

Revised goal: "I want to lose 10 lbs:

It's getting better! It's a relevant goal for them because it applies to their life and will have a significant impact on how that person is able to do things with more ease and confidence.

But will you always want to lose 10 pounds? Is there any urgency to make this happen for you ASAP? After all, today is all we have! If we keep saying we'll start "tomorrow," it'll never happen. So that brings us to the next part of the acronym—Time-bound. You've got to set a deadline to when you're going to achieve your goal.

Revised goal: "I want to lose 10 lbs by tomorrow"

Whoa there, remember that it has to be achievable? Again, love your optimism… but your body is not amazon prime—it will not arrive in 2 days.

Revised goal: "I want to lose 10 lbs in 12 weeks"

Perfect! Now you need an action plan to execute so that you achieve this goal in 12 weeks. You could do this on your own, or get external accountability from an experienced coach who can get you to that goal by doing the right things!

Evaluate your plan every week and see what your progress is. You can weigh yourself, but I also recommend taking weekly progress photos so that you can see your physical body composition changes over time and use it as extra accountability!

Lastly, this goal needs to be recognized or rewarded. You form your habits and actions from what is celebrated in your life! Oh yeah, remember that keg stand you did in college where everyone was cheering for you wildly like hyenas? And then you spent the entire next day throwing up and saying "but it was worth it! I'm a legend!" Yeah. You felt proud because that action was rewarded by external validation from your friends and deep down we all just really want to be liked, right?

So now that you're "grown," find a healthy non-food or drink related way to reward yourself for the goal. Maybe it's buying the wedding dress of your dreams! Maybe it's treating yourself to a vacation to Hawaii where you'll rock your new bikini. Whatever it is, celebrate that shit.

CELEBRATE EVERY ACHIEVEMENT, NO MATTER HOW BIG OR SMALL

Celebrate everything you do like a maniac. This is one of my biggest secret sauce tips to LIFE! Do you ever notice how much time and energy we spend on the negative or whatever seems to not go so well for us? What if we were to all to spend that time and energy on all of the little things we accomplish in life?

Your life would be WAY more enjoyable! That's what would happen!

Right now it's easy for us go through life staring at our bank accounts thinking "why haven't I gotten new clients yet!? Oh no, I haven't signed a new client in a MONTH. Wow, this is a bad month. I'll probably have to get a corporate job again. Then you google corporate jobs for an hour but don't apply to any. Goes back to look at bank account." WHY HAS IT STILL NOT MOVED?!! UGH!! I suck at this!!!

Well, I'll tell you a little something about the universe. It responds to everything you say or think with "yes."

So, your "ugh, I suck!" Mindset will just be confirmed by the universe and the more you say or think that way, the more it'll become your reality.

Instead, what if you can shift your mindset and see and CELEBRATE the good that is happening and have thoughts like this, "I am so grateful for all that I have. My clients love me and I am amazing at what I do. I have a roof over my head and amazing friends who care about me."

And don't just whisper that. I want you to SING THAT!! And PERFORM that affirmation! Dance while you say whatever your affirmation is and feel it on every level of your being!

You went for a run this morning? CELEBRATE IT!

You made a cup of coffee this morning? CELEBRATE IT!

Own every little thing that you do so that you set yourself up for expecting and receiving more of what you want!

When you celebrate something, your brain releases the feel good hormone called Dopamine. The more you celebrate, the better you'll feel and the more good you'll attract into your life. Dance in celebration every single day and your life will get better and better and better.

I want you to be over the top with this! Celebrate every little thing as best as you can for a month and see how it changes your life.

CONNECTING WITH DEEP MOTIVATION

Now the question is this, *why* do you want what you want? Why does your vision fulfill your purpose in life? If you want to be strong and fit enough to keep up with your significant other on a backpacking trip or hiking up a high mountain, if you want to connect with people to feel like you're making a difference in their lives, if you want to find a cure for cancer because you have been through or seen the struggle of loved ones being sick, if you want freedom to travel and find out about other cultures, then *you have* a motivation to go after it. That passion is inside *you*. FEEL IT. Believe that it's there.

The whole idea of this is that your vision is something that resonates with you and makes you feel good about the direction you're going in. If you have a reason to make this vision a reality, then that reason can block all the self-doubt that's flying around in your head.

INTRINSIC MOTIVATION VS. EXTRINSIC MOTIVATION

A lot of people are intrinsically motivated, which means that their reason for doing something comes from within. And a lot of people are extrinsically motivated, which means that they are more motivated by doing something for others. It's important to become familiar with both of these types of motivation to see which one is your main type of motivation.

Most of the time, people have a combination of both of these motivation types. Use one to push the other further.

> **For example**, a goal of losing weight is *intrinsically motivated* by wanting to feel good about yourself and to have high energy during work, play, and sexual relationships. The same goal can be *extrinsically motivated* by wanting others to be attracted to you, to be a good example for your kids and others, and being able to keep up with others on outdoor adventures and at work.

While both motivational factors are at play in your vision, a true vision for oneself is often fueled by a lot of intrinsic motivation. That's because your vision comes from your true self. When you feel that your goals are unappreciated by others, your intrinsic motivation kicks in and can push you regardless of anybody else. This is your true purpose, remember?

FEEDBACK

Gaining motivation is a positive feedback loop. When communicated to others, that intrinsic motivation can be seen by them as motivating and inspiring. Therefore, they support you *more*, encourage you, and build up your confidence by being happy for you that you're doing the right thing. When others are counting on you and encouraging, your intrinsic motivation grows even more. This instilled confidence, when strong enough, can even defeat negativity in the world around you. When someone says that "you can't do it," Your internal fire surges even higher to show them that you can do it and not let the world defeat you. You can do anything! Seriously.

This book is designed to act as a guide through the turmoil that is trying to defeat you and plunge you into helplessness, putting you on a path of freedom that others haven't chosen for you and that your whole heart is excited about.
Are you ready? LET'S GO!

> **Exercise**: Spend 10 minutes lying down with your eyes closed. Visualize your dream and add little pieces to it that not only are part of the whole, but add to the whole. Focus on the main thing you want in life, and how the other things you want are connected to that. They add to each other, culminating in a picture so clear and vibrant that you have goosebumps and a nervous feeling in your throat.

> When a negative or external thought arises, such as the following: "my parents won't be proud of me, my body isn't made to run or be skinny, my job won't let me pursue this," realize that those are safety mechanisms in your brain that want you to

be comfortable and stay on that wide sidewalk that somebody built for you. Push those away and truly focus on that goal you have.

THE POWER OF
COMMUNICATION

"Communication is the solvent of all problems and is the foundation for personal development."

- Peter Shepherd

START
TO LEAD
YOUR LIFE
WITH YOUR
WORDS

I want you to OPEN UP.

Now that you have clarity on your vision, it's time to GO FOR IT! Step 1) Tell everybody about it! Tell everybody around you that you have a goal and tell them why you want it. Tell them with confidence and passion that this dream is what you want and your true self has always wanted it. Opening up like this removes the guarded shell that everybody has and lets your true self shine through. Tell people that you meet at a brewery. Post on social media. Go to events that have people similar to what you want to be. Meet people. BE YOU. And don't apologize for it!

It's natural to feel uncomfortable and nervous when opening up to somebody about anything, let alone a large personal dream. The main reason for this is fear of judgment and rejection.

Sure, you are guaranteed to receive criticism from some people, but realize that they are coming from a place of fear and jealousy. If they are negative, that means that they are on their own wide highway of life that somebody else has paved for them. They are judgmental because they don't realize the possibilities that lie before them, or are too afraid to take the leap that you are taking right now. Use this negativity to fuel yourself, proving others wrong and in the process changing the lives of the doubters by showing them that dreams DO come true.

Look around you. The world is full of highly successful people: entrepreneurs, inventors, athletes, musicians, etc. You know how they made it to where they are? DEDICATION, a PURPOSE, a DRIVE for their goals fueled by heart and an ability to block out the doubters and embrace the support they have around them.

SURROUND YOURSELF WITH THE RIGHT PEOPLE.

The key to gain as much support and motivation for this is to attract the right people into your life to support you and teach you about what it's like to be what you want to be. Opening up to as many people as possible and being inquisitive about their dreams as well makes you realize that everybody has a hidden dream or a next step in life that they want to take.

Growing your network in this way will help you immensely. Not only is it fun to meet people from different walks of life, you can learn from them and get in touch with the exact right people for you. Say, for example, you want to be an actress in Hollywood. Chances are, one of the many people you tell this to has a friend or a relative that lives in Hollywood, or they used to live there and tell you about the movie industry, or they have an idea that will help you get closer to meeting the right people. You would be surprised at the connections you can make by opening up about yourself. It's a small world, after all.

The people that see your enthusiasm and energy for something dear to you will see inspiration, open up to you as well, and give advice and connections to you. The people that respond negatively, however, will keep up their shell and give you reasons why you shouldn't go for it. The only choice you have is to prove them wrong. To limit the negative energy coming from these people, and especially if those are people that are very important in your life, you need to try my three-step method for communication.

THREE-STEP METHOD FOR COMMUNICATION

1. Say what you want- straight up state your goal. Be powerful. Don't waver or say "I think I want to maybe lose 20 pounds or something." Say "I want to lose 20 pounds." Your energy towards this is infectious, and the people who resonate with you will love your enthusiasm.

2. Say why it's important to you - You need a reason for why you're doing this. Say "this is really important to me because I want to be healthier, have more energy, and keep up with our friends on the backpacking trip next summer." Having a reason will make people take you seriously and realize how important this is to you. It also inspires them to think about themselves and how they want to improve or go in a different direction than they're going in. And who doesn't like to inspire others?

3. Appreciate - Be grateful for their support and advice. Not only does it make them feel good about themselves for helping and supporting another person, but it assures continued support.

You can never be too appreciative. Having this level of communication deepens all of your relationships because it takes the guessing out of it. This way, whoever you're communicating with knows exactly how something in particular makes you feel.

CREATING A "BOTH AND"

I used to create separation from my family because of the stories that I made up in my head. I made up the story that all I needed was my boyfriend and that he and I are the only "family" that I need. I thought that my parents didn't support me in my business and that I got all of the love I needed from my boyfriend. Looking back, I can say how ridiculous that is! That is like saying, I only need 99 pieces of love today... I don't want anything else. Get away from me!

LOVE IS INFINITE AND ABUNDANT! I can always create more love to give and receive. I get to allow those in my life and my family to love me. I get to accept their love and give my love to them and be in ABUNDANCE.

What I learned was that comparing the family I was creating to the family I was raised in wasn't healthy. And I get to communicate with my family the stories that I made up in my head and what my request is of them moving forward so that I feel loved and supported in the way that I want to. It gets to be a "BOTH _____ AND _____ ," rather than "EITHER _____ OR _____ ."

We are story creating machines! The more present we can become to our reality and identifying what is simply a story versus reality, the better we can detach from stories that no longer serve us.

LETTING GO OF AVOIDING COMMUNICATION

I've talked to you a lot about the importance of communication—and now I want to talk to you about the importance of letting go of avoidance.

STEPS TO LETTING GO OF AVOIDING COMMUNICATION:

Step 1) Recognize what you are avoiding - Take a second to introspect and ask yourself what you are avoiding. Write it down. Journal about it.

Step 2) Ask yourself why you are avoiding communication - Continue to journal and ask yourself about why you are avoiding communication. Are you afraid of judgment? Are you afraid of someone's reaction? Do you trust the person that you want to communicate with?

Step 3) Decide who you want to talk to - Brainstorm about who can support you with what you're dealing with. Maybe you're ready to communicate to whoever has been directly making you feel a certain way. Or perhaps you'd feel more comfortable calling up someone who's close to you and that you trust like a best friend. Or maybe you decide that you'd like the assistance of a trained 3rd party such as a coach that you can confide in so that you can better process what it is that you've been avoiding.

Step 4) Decide what communication method is right for you - Notice that you can choose to handle avoidance in whatever way feels best for you. Maybe it's writing someone a letter, calling them on the phone, meeting them in person to have a conversation with them about what you've been avoiding... whatever it is, know that you're in control to do whatever feels best for you for where you're at.

Step 5) Execute the method of communication you decided - It's better to communicate in some way than to continue avoiding communicating.

The sooner you communicate what it is that you've

been avoiding—or even denying, the better. For 6 years of my life, I avoided getting help while I was struggling with binge eating disorder. I would experience "calming, dangerous" thoughts in my head, such as "oh it's fine, just eat more" or "you're totally fine, this isn't a problem." I was AFRAID to admit that I had a problem because I didn't want to look weak and admit that I needed help and that I didn't know how to help myself. I have always been someone who wanted to figure things out on my own, but that was actually my biggest weakness. Not being able to accept help from others is what I realized was the problem.

NEGATIVITY

Rejection can be tough to handle. In conversation with others about your vision, in simple life situations where you feel unappreciated, and even in moments of irrational emotional trauma, it always hurts when somebody puts you down. After communicating to your dad, for example, that you want to have a career change, he says that it's not a good idea because your health insurance is important. Even after stating the three step method, he seems to deflect your dream as just that, a dream and not a real possibility. The important thing is to understand that he is trying to keep you safe and protect you by keeping you on the idyllic road to nowhere, and that maybe he is afraid of change because he didn't make a change he wishes he would have in the past.

State again why this is so important to you, and use another amazing communication that I use with my clients: **the clearing method**.

Start by asking your dad if he has a minute to clear with you—this gets his attention and makes sure it isn't a bad time to talk; distractions, time limitations, etc...

Next, state the situation and how it made you feel, the story you made up in your head. For example: "When you brushed off the idea that I have for myself, the story I made up in my head was that I wasn't seen, appreciated, or taken seriously, and that my dreams don't matter compared to other people's."

Your dad, because he loves you and is important to you, wants you to be happy. Seeing that you take this seriously and that your true self is shining through will warrant the support you need to get negative thoughts out of your head. Most likely, there was simply a communication issue and that he believed that what you said was just a passing idea. Communication equals freedom!

These methods of communication work in many areas of life, so don't be afraid to use them when you feel that there is a block in communication.

LIVE YOUR DREAM

Before long, the community you have been seeking will invite you in. If your dream is to be a fashion designer, spreading the word on that will connect you to the right people that can give you advice on how to start. The bigger the network, the more threads in your spiderweb, the better people you meet. You could meet a professor of design at a college near you. You could meet the head of a design company that sees your enthusiasm and talent and invites you to a job interview. You never know! Before you know it, you are surrounded by like minded people that you invited in, giving you the first step towards your goal. If you dream it, you can become it! As the old adage goes: It's not what you know, it's who you know.

Of course, it also helps to know some things. Do your research into what this journey entails. Show what you know in a conversation with others and they'll be even more impressed. These people will teach you even more, and your vision will become even more clear.

Are you starting to feel like you have a lump in your throat just from the thought of having these difficult conversations with people in your life? If you need extra support, reach out. Trust me, I want to see you succeed. What fun is it if all that I wrote is just me talking at you rather than us getting you to implement all of this into your life?

Let's get you extra support. Go to **adriennerivera.com** and schedule a time to speak with me or someone on my team. I'm here for you and I'm so excited for you to start upleveling your communication!

Exercise: Call up one person and have a clearing conversation with them to clear the air between you two. Don't be afraid to let your guard down and be vulnerable. Even though communication can feel really tricky and challenging, it always helps to allow you to understand yourself and others around you better.

BONUS: Use the three step method for communication today, by practicing and asking for what you want in a loving and meaningful way! You've got this!

CREATING HEALTHY RELATIONSHIPS

"For me to stay healthy in a relationship, the individuals have to nurture themselves."

- Anne Heche

SUPPORT OTHERS AND THEY WILL SUPPORT YOU

BEHAVIOR

Behavior is almost always driven by emotion. And emotion is completely driven by relationships! Interactions with others literally change your brain chemistry. As humans, we are social creatures and our minds are designed to learn from and be with other humans. Small moments, such as saying hello on the elevator, raise the amounts of serotonin and dopamine in our brains. Those two things are chemicals that make us happy, and we can get them from many things, including exercise and sociality.

You can find constant examples of emotions controlling actions you take in your life. You make major life changes, like moving to a new city, because your partner got a job there and you heart wants to be with them. You find a job close to your children's school so you can drive them there and spend more time with them. Or small things, like choosing to eat a tub of ice cream after a bad day at work, thinking that the sugar will cause your emotions to switch from frustrated to happy.

So, imagine what BIG moments can do to your brain! Think about a time when you got in a fight with your significant other. That negative energy that was created during the fight stayed with you the entire day, and maybe even as long as a year or longer, right? If you're thinking about a negative experience in your personal life, it becomes impossible to focus on other areas of your life. Many people suffer in their fitness and professional lives because their minds are occupied by thoughts about their relationship. Whereas if your relationships in your life are going well, you can pursue other parts of your life with a full heart. When creating a fitness goal, the first thing you have to do to pursue that goal is to fix your relationships.

START LEARNING FROM THOSE THAT YOU HAVE RESISTANCE TOWARDS

The thing that you DISLIKE about others is a reflection of something in yourself....

How can you get rid of your negative feelings and judgments towards other people? FIRST, notice what triggers you about them. Instead of using that feeling to feel WORSE about yourself, use it as a MIRROR of yourself.

Get real with yourself. Is this a quality in yourself? Does it remind you of something you're trying to suppress, do the opposite of, or are threatened by?

> **EXAMPLE**: A client of mine was resentful towards her husband because he expected her to have the house clean every day.

At the core of this example, the wife feels like the

husband is "stealing some of her independence" and she is being "controlled" and that her husband has "too high of expectations" for her.

So ask yourself, where in your life are YOU too "controlling" of the situation? Where in your life are YOU putting "too high of expectations" on yourself?

Maybe that's stressing you out so much that you're overachieving and compensating in an area of your life, like your job. And then you're using that as an excuse to not take care of yourself because you don't know what workout to do to get results (lack of control) and you think it'll be too hard and take too much time (too high of expectations).

ASK: Who do I NEED TO BE to not let this negatively affect me?

There is good in every situation. There is a lesson to learn in every situation. And bonus points if you can practice the communication skills that you've learned from this book and offer them feedback.

If you were to do this for the above example, you would first ask for their permission to give feedback by saying something along the lines of "I would like to share some feedback about how something that you do makes me feel, is now a good time?" If they say yes, then you can say "Often times when you ask me why I haven't done the dishes, it makes me feel like there are too high of expectations on me and that I'm not acknowledged for everything else that I do. Moving forward, my request to you is that you focus on acknowledging me for what I do get done. Can you honor that request?

Offering them this feedback helps the person that you're giving the feedback know how their actions make you feel. This is a valuable thing for them to learn. It also is valuable to clear the air between you so that there are no resentments built up for how you're interpreting their actions.

BUILDING SUPPORT FOR YOUR FITNESS GOALS

Support from those around you is key to achieving those fitness goals. And those people need a positive relationship with you in order to support you. What better way to create a positive relationship than with communication and vulnerability?

Communication, as I've mentioned before, is such a key in every relationship. If you tell those around you how important those goals you have in a vulnerable, real way, then they will band around you and cheer you on to no end. Tell people what you're thinking! Tell people what stories you made up in your head because of support or lack of support you've received from them. The only way to solve problems or sticking points in your relationship to others is to communicate them openly and take them on head first. Use my 3-step method that I shared with you from chapter 2 and go for it.

Many times, if you have a story in your head that others don't support you in your dreams, simply communicating this will dispel all of these myths. Others simply didn't know about these goals or didn't realize the level of support you wanted.

UNAPOLOGETICALLY START ASKING FOR HELP

Asking for help is an important part of this, and is hard for many people. You are WORTHY of having support in your life. Forget about the story you've created in your head that makes you think that you asking for support is taking from someone. It's not taking at all, it's giving. Give those around you the gift of clarity for what you really want and how it will make you feel. Trust me, those in your life that really love you will LOVE to know specific things that they can do to show you that they love you more often. It feels good to help others, so allow others to enjoy helping you out.

Both partners in any relationship are EQUAL. This means you get to both ask for help and give help. When you communicate what you want to others, and truly open up and be curious about them, they can open up to you about what they want in life as well. When you help others and offer your advice, point of view, and life experience to them, OF COURSE they will offer that to you as well.

An encouraged person is always one who is willing to give encouragement. Spread the love to those around you and you will receive love from them as well. With positive relationships around you, you will feel more energized, happier, and driven to pump that iron!

COMMUNITY

Building your community starts with your loved ones around you. Support that you give to others reflects back onto you, and community can blossom bigger and more beautifully than you can imagine. With everybody supporting each other, nobody feels alone and everybody feels as if their dreams can be realized. The reason for this is accountability.

Having a friend meet you at 5 in the morning at the park to run is a lot more motivating than having to go alone. Even just telling your friends that you're getting up before work to go to the gym makes you feel as if they're counting on you, and so you actually go! Working together towards a common goal is a way to make individual goals happen, too. Like-minded people surrounding you is a beautiful thing.

Another way to add accountability is to have a coach to cheer you on as well as provide insight into what exactly goes into realizing your goals. Also, going to group fitness classes is a way to meet other strong people and work together with them in an organized environment.

One of my clients, Rianne, said that she had no idea how helpful it was to have our supportive Facebook community during my No Added Sugar Challenge. She had tried to do it on her own before but never followed through. She said that having everyone else post that they were also having temptations made her feel normal and motivated to stick to it because everyone else was having cravings and not giving into them.

A sense of camaraderie and healthy competition helps our clients accomplish their goals and have fun while doing it.

> **EXERCISE**: Have a support conversation! Think of someone that you are in relationship with, perhaps a significant other. Ask them to have a conversation with you to learn about each other's goals and how you can support one another. Start by being person number 1 and share your goals with person number 2. Then have person number 2 ask how they can support you and tell person number 2 all of your requests for them, giving them loving and constructive feedback on what hasn't been

helpful in the past. Allow them to reflect and ask them if they can honor that request. After you are complete, person number 1 will switch with person number 2.

YOUR RELATIONSHIP WITH <u>FITNESS</u>

"If you can't fly, then run, If you can't run, then walk, If you can't walk, then crawl, but whatever you do, you have to keep moving forward."

– Martin Luther King Jr.

Working out is one thing, your mindset around working out is another

HOW NUTRITION AFFECTS YOUR FITNESS

What you put into your body on a nutritional level has a large impact on how fitness feels in your body. Food fuels us and gives us energy to feel STRONG during workouts, which makes a big difference mentally in how working out feels in our bodies.

You could go from eating poorly and thinking that working out is horribly hard and wipes out all of your energy, or you could show up to the gym and crush your workout because you have the energy to show up 100%. Option 2 makes you leave feeling challenged and full of endorphins.

At the most basic level, food is energy. Therefore, if the foods that we're eating are energetically heavy or don't agree well with our bodies, they weigh us down. For example, let's say that you know that you are lactose intolerant but you're still eating pizza and ice cream. Then your body has to do extra work to get it out of your body because it cannot properly digest it.

I want you to ask yourself; what foods are you still eating that constantly make you feel bad in your body? I'm not talking about guilt, but about feelings of heaviness, bloating, and just not agreeing with your system. WHY ARE YOU STILL EATING THESE FOODS? Food is energy! And energy is feedback for us. We get to listen to the feedback that our body receives from the food that we eat.

It's like going on a first date. If your date's energy doesn't click and align with yours, then do you think you'd still go out on a date with that person once a week forever? I hope not!! Food is the same way.

Your body is smart. Listen to what it has to teach you about itself. Your body is uniquely yours. Even "healthy" foods like apples may not agree with your stomach. I want you to empower yourself to be your own biggest teacher. It doesn't matter what the textbook says about a certain food, how the certain food makes you FEEL is way more important and is valuable feedback for you.

If we continue to be blindsided to the things that don't agree with our body, we become lethargic and this impacts how we show up in every area of our lives. This weighs down our energy and slows down our vibration. Your body is literally the vessel that houses your soul. It is your DUTY to treat it in the way that you value your own worth.

How worthy are you? You are worthy of housing your soul in a CASTLE of a body—so be present to treating it in that way from the inside out. What are you consuming? And does what you are consuming make you feel how you want to feel? (Note: This includes the media and information that you're consuming too!) If we have the ability to eat, then we have the ability to

CHOOSE what we eat and choose what feels best in our physical body as well as our souls.

What would it be like if you shifted your mindset into seeing each and every meal as something sacred? All meals should be sacred. A meal is so special when you think about where all of the ingredients came from to make it onto your plate and all of the hands that helped out to harvest all of the ingredients. Gratitude is healing. Slow down and breathe in the gratitude that you have before the next meal—I promise it'll make the food taste better too!

SPIRITUAL CONNECTION OF FITNESS + NUTRITION

Life is about the mind + body + spirit connection. We are designed to move our bodies and exercise! And just like with anything, you can do too much of one thing. What is the best fitness thing out there? The answer: there isn't just one! I teach yoga, spin class, high intensity interval training, Pilates, and I also am a personal trainer. And because of that, I see the benefits in ALL types of fitness—but I also see the negative impacts that any one thing can have on the body.

For example, a lot of my clients come to me as avid yogis and they aren't getting the results that they want. While yoga is great for flexibility and spirituality, it's not ideal for weight loss. And a lot of the time in Vinyasa

Yoga classes, there can be too many forward folds and child's poses—both of which flatten the low back and can cause low back pain or pain in the glutes. Your glutes can become underactive from being lengthened for a long time as well.

While yoga has a lot of amazing benefits, you can do too much of it and it's best to also do cardio and strength training to balance the body.

FINDING THE BALANCE IN DOING WHAT YOU LOVE

What if you just LOVE running or playing volleyball? Would it be okay just to do the fitness that makes you the happiest? Well let me ask you this. Have you ever been on a sports team or viewed a team practice before? Every single one of them includes cross-training to balance the body. If you were to just run, then chances are you would be out of balance and overuse certain muscles which could result in injury. For example, doing lateral band walks help to strengthen the outer glute muscles, which help to keep the knee in line with your hip and ankle. This is very important for proper running form.

SEEING THE GYM AS A SPIRITUAL PLACE

You get to do a mix of physical activity to find balance. My goal for you is to find a spiritual connection in anything that you do to move your body. Even in the gym, you can connect to your breath and your body to become more connected to yourself. What are your preexisting beliefs about the gym? Do you already see it as a spiritual place? Perhaps you don't resonate with it yet, and if that's the case, think about your favorite type of exercise and ask yourself what you like about it. And recreate that aspect of it in the gym.

Example: I love volleyball because of the team aspect!

Mindset Shift: I get to cheer on others in the gym and do my best workout so that I can motivate others by leading by example.

Example: I love yoga because of connecting my body to my breath

Mindset Shift: I get to connect my breath to my muscles when lifting weights. As I exhale my breath when I go up in a squat, I squeeze my glutes and am present to the muscles that I'm working.

Fitness is ALL about mindset and working on your fitness impacts every other area of your life! Take it from my client, Rachel.

Rachel said, "I know a lot of times it can feel intimidating to commit and dive into something like this with yourself and to really be showing up for things like working out, paying attention to your diet and looking at your mindset. Going into it, I felt kind of scared. It felt more accessible working with you."

Rachel said that before working with me, she used to think that going to the gym needed to be a punishment for herself.

She feared that she wasn't WORTHY of investing the time and money into herself. And she found that the more that she did work on herself and invest in herself, the more everything else in her life became much better.

BE SELFISH

We are taught that putting yourself first and caring for yourself before others is a bad thing. That's totally backwards. We can only give as much as we are able to receive. The energy in our bodies becomes drained if we are always giving and not finding balance between giving and receiving.

You all know the phrase, "you can't pour from an empty cup!" It's actually truly SELFISH to not take care of yourself first because then you're limiting the fullness of energy and love that you have to overflow and give to everyone else. Knowing that you're worthy of time for yourself and deciding to do things for yourself brings you to a place of abundance where there is more than enough time and an overflow of love to give.

Exercise: Repeat these Mindset Affirmations daily!

1. I have an abundance of healthy and nourishing food that I get to eat whenever I'm hungry.
2. I am in control and present with everything that I eat and every workout that I do.
3. Food is to nourish me. Therefore, I am thankful for food.
4. Exercise makes me strong. Therefore, I love moving my body daily.
5. I get to be in control of what I decide to do with my cravings.
6. I will never feel restricted or unsatiated and I will eat until I'm full.
7. I will honor my emotions without using food as a coping mechanism.
8. I am worthy of being nourished. Therefore, my meals and my fitness routine reflect that.
9. I exercise because I love my body for where I am at NOW on the journey. Exercise is for my soul, and I am worthy of challenging myself.
10. I will eat consistently throughout the day to keep my mind and body plenty nourished and energized.

LEARNING TO LOVE YOURSELF

"You are perfect. To think anything less is as pointless as a river thinking that it's got too many curves or that it moves too slowly or that its rapids are too rapid. Says who? You're on a journey with no defined beginning, middle or end. There are no wrong twists and turns. There is just being. And your job is to be as you as you can be. This is why you're here. To shy away from who you truly are would leave the world you-less. You are the only you there is and ever will be. I repeat, you are the only you there is and ever will be. Do not deny the world its one and only chance to bask in your brilliance."

- Jen Sincero

What do
you say to
yourself in the
mirror when
no one else is
watching?

WHAT IS YOUR RELATIONSHIP WITH YOURSELF?

You may have heard the phrase "you can't pour from an empty cup" or "you can't love others as much as you love yourself." I believe that this is partially true— let me explain.

For the majority of my life, I was a huge people pleaser. I wanted to make EVERYONE happy and make EVERYONE feel that they were always right and loved. And while you may say, well yes, you have a big heart—what's wrong with that?

You simply can't be EVERYTHING to EVERYONE in life or else you'll burn out or lose time for YOU. And if you're always taking care of everyone else, who is going to take care of you? You get to take care of you— you are WORTHY of it.

It's just like on an airplane—they always say to put on your oxygen mask first. Yes, doing things for others is amazing, BUT imagine how much more love and presence you'd have to give to your loved ones if you "filled your own cup" first.

SELF-FORGIVENESS

In order to truly love yourself, you have to first learn to forgive yourself. No one is perfect. We've all messed up big time at some point in our lives. We've said the wrong things or have done actions out of selfishness. I believe that there is no worse feeling in the world that you can have than emotionally hurting others.

Here's the thing—I've been there. I remember being on the playground in 3rd grade wanting to play with new friends. My normal playground buddy came over to me and I told her I didn't want to play with her today and she went behind a tree and cried. I didn't know how to make her feel better!

Over the years, I've had moments where I've made worse decisions. I became the bully that I used to fear in others. I took out my pain and inner-frustrations on those around me that I loved the most. I hated that part of me—I hated her until I learned all that she taught me.

I learned that I just wanted to have a voice! I wanted to own my power! I wanted to have LOVE. All humans need LOVE. We deserve it no matter what! It's not about your mistakes, it's about how you grow from them and move forward with your life.

I've found that both in my life and with my clients, often times the people that we hurt the most and the ones that we love the most. The reason for this is because they are SAFE, they are always going to love us no matter what, so it seems. They can be our rawest form of a target to unleash ourselves on.

And most of the time, they do forgive you. Whether they forgive you or not, it is always hardest to forgive yourself.

But at the end of the day, forgiveness is a choice! You get to decide that you are WORTHY of freeing yourself from whatever bad names you've been sabotaging yourself with.

POWER OF FORGIVING OTHERS

Not being able to forgive someone does not help you. It's only making you live with hundreds of pounds of baggage that you just need to release for your soul to feel lighter and happier.

In my life, I've tried so hard to forgive the people in my life that have hurt me the most. What has helped me is asking myself, "what did I gain from that relationship, how has this experience strengthened me more, or how can I detach from what happened and be neutral about the situation."

There's definitely people out there that might be really hard to forgive because you strongly disagree with what decisions they've made. And at the same time, you get to think about your own mental health and what it would look like for you to detach from their actions and release the need to take it personally. If you're taking on the weight of the world, you're going to have extra stress that doesn't serve you.

You may allow yourself permission to release the need to worry about it because it's not your life. It's a projection of the other person's life. Nothing in the world is your fault, or anyone's fault. It simply just is the way that things happened; practice seeing them with a neutral mind.

People's actions are simply a byproduct from what they are mentally going through and all the stress that they're feeling with multiple areas of their life. It's part of your mental HEALTH to forgive others and it's also worth noting that you can forgive someone while still keeping them out of your life.

Think of someone that you still need to forgive. Say out loud "I forgive you, but I need to keep some distance for my own love for myself because I get to respect my boundaries. I forgive you because you made me a strong person and because some good has come out of every bad situation even if it feels horrible." It makes you stronger, shows you what not to be like, and it makes you able to endure anything in life.

Once you release what has been weighing you down energetically, you will have a much easier time releasing the weight physically. Often times people use food as a way to cope and suppress past and present traumas, fears, and beliefs. Whatever your vice is, ask yourself how it's supporting you and how to get rid of it. It is important to release that weight that you're carrying of the responsibility to make someone be a certain way.

WORTHINESS

YOUR SELF-WORTH DETERMINES YOUR SELF-LOVE.

An affirmation that I use frequently with myself as well as with my clients is, "I am worthy simply because I breath." This means that just because you are alive you are worthy. Often times we start to try to equate our worthiness to our income, what we do, or our past--none of those are in the equation. You have been created by the universe and that is a huge gift! You are worthy simply because you've been born.

SELF-TALK

What you say to yourself when you look in the mirror is important. Are you hard on yourself? Do you love yourself?

Often times on my FREE initial discovery calls that I have with clients before I start working with them, they tell me that when they look in the mirror, the first thing that they see is the rolls on their stomach and their thick thighs.. They *hate* the body that they are living in.

I want to teach you how to LOVE your body and your mind from the inside out! You are worthy of loving yourself exactly as you are.

> **MINDSET SHIFT**: I want to inspire you to fall in love with your body so that you shift from the thought "I need to lose 10 pounds because I hate the way I look" to "I am so grateful that I have a body. I love myself so much that I am WORTHY of conquering my fitness goals and getting stronger. "

MINDSET IS THE KEY TO SELF-LOVE

Start to become aware of your mindset. Just start to *listen* to your thoughts. What are your thoughts like? What core things do you spend your day thinking about? What *do* you say in your head when you look in the mirror? The most inner awareness you can have for yourself--the better. If you know where you're at, you can identify any gaps and see how to bridge them.

Once you start to realize these thoughts use the **Red Light, Yellow Light, Green Light Method.**

> **Step 1**. Pause and stop after you notice a negative thought running through your head.

Step 2. Decide what you are going to do with that thought. This is your chance to shift into being nice towards yourself and to be optimistic.

Step 3. Rewrite that thought! Simply rewind for a second, put your pointer finger up in the air and draw a circle with a slash through it and say "cancel thought." Then you say (in your head or out loud) what you meant to say and what you shifted into.

MANAGING OTHER PEOPLE'S PERCEPTIONS

One of Don Miguel Ruiz's 4 Agreements is to not take things personally. This is so simple yet it keeps so many of us stuck living this way. We start living for the approval of our parents, friends, and neighbors rather than tuning in with ourselves and asking ourselves what we really want out of life. It's okay if certain people or their wants aren't a part of your vision. Remember back to all of Chapter 1! Your vision is yours—it's always been inside you. The outside noise from everyone else has just been distracting you.

It's okay to disagree. And it's much more rewarding for a number of people to really love you for you and have some people not like you than to have everyone just be okay with you. Be you! By holding back on truly being yourself, you are robbing the world of the gift of what it's like to have you!

RELEASING PAST TRAUMAS

Love yourself by realizing all the experiences you've had that make you who you are today. Past traumas make you stronger. You are worthy of your goals just like everybody else is. Nobody has special rights or is better than anyone, successful people are just people who have gone after their goals and loved themselves.

Allow yourself to shift your mindset from being in a victim story to having compassion for those in your life that have hurt you. It may be challenging to allow yourself to do this, but it will take loads off of you. It's a choice to have compassion for others.

Do the inner work to own your worth and truly start loving yourself as you are. If you are noticing that you have past traumas in your life that are affecting your thoughts, how you see the world, and yourself—I recommend talking to a trained psychologist or therapist. It doesn't happen overnight, but you'll be happy that you did and continue to do the inner work to break through.

Speaking of breakthroughs, I hope you're gaining a lot of insight into how you view yourself, your goals, and your life. If you haven't scheduled a time to talk with me or someone on my team, do it! Accept guidance. I love you and would love to help you start integrating what you're learning to your life.

STEPS TO LOVING YOURSELF:

1.) Know Your Worth: A mantra that I love using myself is "I am worthy simply because I breathe." Often times, we spend our lives trying to improve ourselves SO THAT we will then become worthy.

This is so backwards. We often think, "once I make a million dollars, I will be worthy"—this thought does nothing but keep us never feeling fulfilled or happy. You get to shift into, "I am so worthy of accomplishing anything I want in life." You are already WORTHY!! Declare your worth today and the universe will provide for you.

2.) Celebrate Yourself: Celebrate yourself for being YOU. When you are living life from a place of love, everything works in your favor. Express yourself and celebrate yourself for who you already are! The final secret to loving yourself is seeing yourself as that beautiful and amazing person that you already are. Love yourself for the heart that you have… that is beating right now, full of love for others in the world.

How does it feel to "try on" the idea that each and every time your heart beats, it's generating more love in the world. Love is always increasing exponentially.

3.) Live Your Life for Your Purpose: Discover what

lights you up. Discover your purpose in life. How can you support others? When we are living in love for others, we create more love for ourselves.

The first step is always putting yourself first. As you take care of your own needs, you will create more space to support and love others.

Exercise: Every time you get out of the shower, say something loving to yourself. Appreciate that you have a body! I challenge you to show extra love through your thoughts and actions to the parts of yourself that you used to be the meanest to. You get to start working on your relationship with yourself.

BONUS: Open your journal and write yourself a letter of self-compassion. Free yourself of judgment towards the things that you wish you had or hadn't done. Start with choosing an aspect of yourself that you currently criticize or perhaps don't like. Imagine someone who is free of judgment and overflowing with love. Write a letter to yourself from this friend. Set the letter aside and then in 15+ minutes come back and reread the letter. Let the words truly sink in. Keep this letter on your night stand or somewhere that you see it often as a reminder to come back to reread it.

BUILDING A HEALTHY RELATIONSHIP WITH <u>FOOD</u>

"What you need is some balance in your life: to know when to say no and when to say yes, how to ask for help as easily as you give it, when to let other people live with the consequences of their choices, how to be honest with yourself (always) and forthright and direct with other people (most of the time), and why it's important to give up striving to be perfect and accept your perfectly imperfect self."

- Karen R. Koenig

NOURISH YOUR BODY BECAUSE YOU'RE WORTHY OF IT

What is your relationship with food?

What if we pause for a second and detach from all of the media out there on specifically what to eat and what not to eat? What is the mindset you have attached around the act of eating certain foods? What are the thoughts that run through your head while eating? Do you feel guilt after eating? We get to dive deep and look into all of these things in this chapter.

ABUNDANCE EATING

What if food was simply just that—food? This is the mindset that I want to introduce you to. This is a mindset that I've coined as the term "abundance eating"— which I will be diving further into in this chapter. Food is simply just food—simply just made of calories. The only difference between one food and the next food is how many nutrients it has in it. The simpler we make it, the better.

WHY DO WE OVER-COMPLICATE FOOD? FOOD IS FOOD

What's the benefit to seeing food as simply just food? When we detach from the guilt and shame that we attach around eating or the choices that we make with certain foods, we can let go of "mental calories."

What are "mental calories?" What I mean when I refer to "mental calories" is that the guilt we feel towards a certain food adds more calories to the food that we just ate by adding stress to it. For example, you can have a 100 calorie cookie, enjoy it and release guilt around it. In that case, it's just 100 calories. But if you experience guilt, that cookie creates more stress in your body and "adds calories."

Guilt brings more stress to your body. Cortisol is a stress hormone that is released in your body when you're stressed. This could be the science behind "mental calories" and why it seems that those that experience a lot of judgmental thoughts around food keep more excess weight on.

So are "mental calories" actually a thing? Well if you looked in the National Academy of Sports Medicine Personal Training Book, you definitely wouldn't find that term. What they would say is weight loss is as simple as being in a caloric deficit and that that's the only way to lose weight.

You and I know that stress has an impact on the body, so if we can take off some pressure from ourselves and enjoy all foods in moderate portions, then we'll feel so much better. And by the way, you never have to diet again!

Once you master the mindset around food, people will be asking you what you've been doing to have gained such control in every area of your life! Be the example of what it's like to live a life of food freedom.

HOW TO MANAGE YOUR CRAVINGS AROUND FOOD

Have you ever had cravings? Of course you have! Because we're all human, right! Whether it's a margarita after work, a muffin for breakfast or late night chocolate, we'll all had cravings before. But the secret about craving is that it's all about mindset.

You never want to feel restricted. That's why as a coach, I never tell my clients things like, "you're not allowed to eat this, you're on a DIET, I'm disappointed in you for eating that." Do you remember when a parental figure in your life told you that you weren't allowed to do something? Then you found a way to sneak around and do it because the inner child in you simply wanted FREEDOM. That inner child screams, "You can't tell me what to do! It's my life, I run the show!"

We've all been there, and that's why I know that if I were to tell you what foods you couldn't eat that that's not going to help you. I'm simply your guide to give you the tools to make the biggest changes that you can for where you're at in your life. I want you guys to be honest with yourselves and others! Let's say that you're working with me and you're struggling with a certain craving, I want you to know that it's safe to tell me. I want you to know that when you tell me what you're dealing with, you're holding yourself accountable AND it's no longer a secret.

DO YOU HAVE FOOD SECRETS?

When I was dealing with binge eating disorder for 6 years of my life, it thrived because it was in secrecy. I was hiding what I was eating and because of that it felt scary. I felt completely out of control, and regained control only once I opened up and made everyone in my living situation aware that I was struggling with binge eating disorder and my requests for them to support me. I told them that I requested for them to not make any comments about what I was eating or how much I was eating.

Currently, I live with my significant other. He knows that this is something that I used to struggle with. And he knows in order to keep me free of binge eating disorder, all he has to do is not make any comments about what I'm eating. I need the freedom and control to know that the foods that I eat are my choice. For example, if he were to tell me that I wasn't allowed to eat chocolate or that I shouldn't keep eating food then I would feel restricted. And if I felt that way, then I'd want sneak down to the kitchen after he goes to bed and eat everything in spite of him!

Make a promise to yourself right now that you'll

communicate to EVERYONE in your current household how they can best communicate with you in order to best support you. When you tell your family, it may be the same as when I told mine or it could be completely different. What I told my family is "I don't want to feel judged and told what I should and shouldn't eat. I want to be able to eat whatever I want in front of you so that it's no longer a secret and an issue, can you support me in giving me space and freedom to eating what I want?"

3 CHOICES WHEN YOU'RE HAVING A CRAVING

Let's say you just got home from work and you're really craving a glass of wine. In this example, you have the following 3 choices:

1. GIVE IN - You want the glass of wine so you have the glass of wine

2. RESIST THE URGE - I really want that wine, ugh! I'm gonna try AS HARD AS I CAN NOT TO HAVE IT!!! I'm going crazy!!!

3. ALLOW THE URGE & DON'T GIVE IN - You allow yourself to be uncomfortable and know that the feeling will pass and you exercise your willpower to not give in

Which one do you think is the correct choice? Number 3! Ding, ding, ding! We have a winner! This is a challenge at first. It's challenging to sit in discomfort and allow it—especially in today's society where nearly everything in life is geared towards making things simple and comfortable for us. The easy part of this is not giving in!

It's not actually hard to not have a glass of wine. That's easy! It's easy to not do it, you simply say no! It's just like not feeding your dog Frito's for dinner. It's easy to decide to feed him his dog food every night. What is difficult is feeling that feeling inside of you when you tell yourself "no."

EXERCISING YOUR WILLPOWER

It's like the kid that we've all seen in the grocery store. He's walking with his mom and he screams, "I want a donut! Mommy, please can I have it!" The mom tells the son no and that it's okay. And the child starts crying and making a big scene while the mom simply ALLOWS her son to feel the brief sense of discomfort, knowing that soon it will pass.

The way to use this analogy on yourself is to "step out of our your body" and visualize the inner child inside you having a temper tantrum. You have compassion for your inner child and you tell your inner child that it's going to be okay. Know that it's okay if you're feeling physical stress in your body. Step outside of how you're feeling in your body and without any judgments say "hmm, isn't that interesting." You get to tell yourself, "it's okay. Feel this way as long as you need, I'm not resisting you. I'm simply allowing you and I'm your observer.

THERE IS NO "GOOD AND BAD"

Here's the thing, it's not that food is "bad." Donuts aren't "bad," there is no "good and bad," just foods that simply have more nutrients. What we are addressing here is not the food, it's the act of giving in. So instead, what you should do is plan out your cravings rather than giving in to them.

Write this down: Instead of giving in to my cravings, I simply schedule them out.

That's all you have to do! You're not saying "no" to your craving forever, you're just saying "I'll eat this later." If you're craving a muffin at a coffee shop, plan it for 2 days later and treat yourself then.

THE PSYCHOLOGY BEHIND YOUR CRAVINGS

Have you heard of the famous psychology experiment with Pavlov's dogs? He rang the bell every time the dogs would eat. And eventually he started to ring a bell and found that soon enough, just the ringing of the bell would make the dogs salivate. The dogs thought that food was coming simply because they associated getting fed with the ringing of the bell.

Let's say that this is how you are. Maybe once it's midnight you're hungry and still up working, so you crave a piece of chocolate. And you are used to having the chocolate to help keep you awake. (Pause for a second. If it's late, do you really need to continue working that late? Sleep is one of the most important things that we can do! It repairs our mind and helps us to recover our muscles. Prioritize sleep and don't stay up to the point where you're having the late night cravings in the first place).

Anyways, imagine that the clock that strikes midnight is the ringing of the bell. And that bell is saying, "come on, it's midnight. Time for chocolate!" And every bone in your body is nearly lifting you up out of your chair to go and give in to your craving. But you don't have to! You do have self-control and it's like a muscle. It gets stronger the more that you exercise it! You get to DECIDE that you do have willpower and that you're going to start using it.

If you were to continue ringing the bell for the dogs and continue to not give them food, they would learn soon enough that the bell no longer means food is coming and they'd no longer salivate and have that urge. It's the same with you! Once you decide that you're going to exercise willpower and allow yourself to feel discomfort, then you start to undo that learned habit.

DECIDING TO COMMIT TO YOUR GOALS

This is exactly what happened the first time I led a "No Added Sugar Challenge." The reason why I led the 31 Days of No Added Sugar challenge was because I realized that I needed it! There had been a lot of summer BBQ's and sugar was starting to control me (it acts like a drug in your brain). It was the most challenging thing to do, but once you really COMMIT to doing it, you no longer crave sugar and you break that habit and addiction. Some of my clients that did the challenge started to see physical changes within the first few days! Other clients took about 3 weeks before they started to no longer crave sugar.

The biggest thing that I found for me was how emotional I was the first 3 days. I cried every single day and I loved every second of it! I didn't realize that I typically went to sugar as a pick-me-up. Without it, I sat with my actual emotions and got to the core of what I was dealing with and allowed myself to feel sad, bad, and crappy. It's HEALTHY to confront our emotions and dig deep to find out what's going on deep within. Throughout the 31 days, I felt like I have better focus, more energy and I'm more toned!

Sometimes just the thought of saying no to our biggest

cravings can feel really challenging. Maybe you're really doubting your ability to control those urges. Maybe you're thinking, "oh it's easy for her to say. She has more willpower than me." That's simply not the case. There are many tips and tricks that I teach in my one-on-one and group coaching to "trick your brain" into extinguishing those cravings in the heat of the moment. Go to **adriennerivera.com** to learn more about our coaching program.

LANGUAGE AROUND FOOD

I want you to be mindful with the way that you're talking about food to yourself. Notice if you are saying to yourself anything along the lines of "you CAN'T have carbs," or "you're NOT ALLOWED to eat sugar." Are you restrictive to yourself through your language around food?

I was recently on a coaching call with a client about this. She said "this weekend I didn't really adhere to my diet..." And I pointed out that she's not on a diet. I give my clients the option to track food based on their current and past mindsets around food. For some of my clients that like having structure, having a calorie and macro goal for food can be very beneficial to getting them steady results. Tracking calories doesn't mean you're on a diet. Of course I make recommendations on which foods to have an abundance of AND—if you go out and have a croissant, it's okay! Enjoy it and enjoy life. You get to find balance in your life to see the results that you want to in life.

SHIFT YOUR MINDSET AROUND FOOD

If you're struggling with consistency around nutrition, it's because you aren't actually fully committed. If that's the case, you get to tune into the reason "WHY" nutrition is important to you. And you know what they say, your "why" should make you cry... it should really hit DEEP into your heart. Your reason why nutrition is important for you isn't so that you can simply feel better. It's more likely so that you can feel your best to live a long life and be active with your kids and easily take them on adventures! Really dig deep into why you're committed to fitness and nutrition. Sometimes it's challenging to discover your "why" by yourself. If you'd like support, go to my website **adriennerivera. com** and contact me there. Let me know that you'd like support finding your why.

In order to shift your mindset around food, you get to shift the way you talk to yourself about food. Stop using the word "diet," diets are temporary and they don't work. COMMIT to a lifestyle that you can commit to. Another thing to become aware of is your judgments around food. Are you judging yourself or the food itself? Are you having thoughts such as, "why did you eat that! You'll never lose weight," chances are that you're adding an unnecessary amount of stress to yourself that's not serving you. Have compassion for yourself. Start to remove the negatives in your language around food and instead think of the positives of what you get to have more of. And if you're going to have a cookie, please please please enjoy it 100%!

> **MINDSET BEFORE**: "I need this cappuccino because I'm really tired. It's the only way to give me energy and I'm craving it so much."

> **MINDSET SHIFT**: "I love myself so much that I can refrain from this. And in fact, I'm being so mindful right now that I think I'm having this craving for chocolate because I'm really exhausted from all that I've done today. I'll take a power nap and rest up to recharge my body with the sleep that it needs."

FINDING BALANCE WITH FOOD

What does having balance with food actually look like? Well, truthfully it looks different for different people based on their goals, their past, and their current mindset. For some people, this may take small changes such as having less alcoholic beverages or sodas. For others, maybe you never have soda or alcohol and that isn't something that you need assistance fine tuning.

What I do recommend is creating healthy boundaries with yourself around food and alcohol. Be honest with yourself and ask yourself what is realistic for yourself and is in alignment with your goals? For example, perhaps creating healthy boundaries looks like allowing yourself to have 2 alcoholic drinks per week as a maximum. Listen to what feels doable for you for where you're at right now. Create your own healthy boundaries that push you just outside of your comfort zone and show you what you're capable of.

DON'T BE AFRAID TO TEST YOUR WILLPOWER.

You have more willpower than you think!! You are strong! Even if you feel highly compulsive towards certain things, the truth is you'd be okay without them.

MASTERING MINDSET + MOTIVATION

"Start by doing what's necessary; then do what's possible; and suddenly you're doing the impossible."

– Francis of Assisi

YOUR MIND CREATES YOUR REALITY

YOUR THOUGHTS CREATE YOUR REALITY AND WHO YOU ARE

If you haven't caught on yet, this entire book has been about your mindset through the lens of everything in your life being a relationship!

There is so much that goes into mindset, and mindset mastery is an ongoing process that requires a lifetime of learning and growing, In this chapter, I will provide you with the basics of becoming more aware of your mindset so that you can begin to shift and grow in the right direction.

ARE YOU OPERATING OUT OF FEAR OR FROM LOVE?

As Marianne Williamson always says, the opposite of love is fear. Being in a state of fear is a mindset of scarcity. Being in this state creates thought such as "there will never be enough time or money or love," instead of operating from a state of love and abundance and knowing and really realizing and believing that there is an overflow of love and abundance in the world.

I USED TO OPERATE FROM A PLACE OF FEAR.

Rewind back to the first retreat that I ever went on.

I had been free from binge eating for 3 years. I had found ways to find comfort in learning how to fully love myself, helping others, teaching fitness classes, and through self-care. I was in a really good place, BUT I was dealing with a constant "pain in my stomach." It was fear. It was anxiety. It was stress that had been bottled up inside me. I didn't know how to let it go! I am a strong believer that things happen for a reason, and that week I was invited to a river retreat. It turned out to be a week where I didn't have work and I had no excuse not to go.

We rafted down the river to our new home for the retreat.

And by "new home," I mean a "campground" that we would be staying at for the next few days. And by "campground," I mean "dusty dirt ground that was infested with millions of ants."

For those of you who don't know, I always used to be SUPER TERRIFIED of bugs and ants.

When I got off the raft and went further into the woods, I was practically running in place so that I didn't have the ants crawl up my legs. I didn't know how I was going to survive the retreat. I had a HUGE fear of ants. But I also knew that I was ready to let go of my fears. That night, we sat at the picnic tables and it got dark. I didn't feel the ants crawling up my legs...

They were out of sight, out of mind. This eased my anxiety.

The next day, we had a "cacao ceremony." This was where everyone had a cup of cacao (essentially real hot chocolate) in their hands. Our retreat leader instructed us to hold the cup in our hands, feel the warmth, smell the cacao, and envision ourselves putting an intention into the cacao.

And at this moment, I literally broke out in fear. My old fears around food were wanting to resurface.

I had never been so mindful with food. Breaking through the resistance I had by actually having patience brought up a lot of old feelings from when I was dealing with binge eating disorder. I put on my sunglasses to try to avoid anyone from seeing my tears, for I had fear of being judged instead of loved.

We paired up with someone in the group that we didn't know very well to share our experiences with the cacao ceremony. He kindly asked me to take off my sunglasses before I shared. As soon as I did, I broke out crying and all I could say was "I'm dealing with a lot of fears." And I sat there, still crying for the remaining 4 minutes that I had to share, thinking silently to myself of all of the fears that I had ever dealt with.

My thoughts went something like this:

> "I've been fearing that there isn't enough…. Enough time, enough food, enough support"
> "I've been fearing expressing myself… I've only shown anger like 3 times in my life, since I grew up thinking it was not an okay emotion to have"
> "I've been fearing feeling safe…"
> "I've been fearing trusting myself… trusting myself to make the right decisions and to have confidence in them"

The list went on and on.

After that, we had a "water healing ceremony," where everyone was standing in a circle on the edge of the river, which was 2 feet deep. Everyone had 30 seconds to do whatever they wanted in the center, and then everyone placed a hand on them for 30 seconds.

I KNEW THAT I WAS READY TO RELEASE ALL OF THE FEAR I HAD BEEN HOLDING ONTO

When it was my turn, I released my fear of the cold water by face-planting into the water and screaming underwater with rage!! I did this with the intention of releasing any feeling of anger that I had ever suppressed.

I rolled over and floated, panting, with adrenaline rushing through me. My eyes were closed, and suddenly 18 hands were placed on me, the last hand placed on my stomach... where I had been holding all of my fear.

I started to hyperventilate as my stomach went up and down.

It was as if their hands had lifted the fear out of my body. It was as if all of these strangers/ new friends were my angels.

In that moment, I realized that I have angels all around me. The person who bags my groceries is my angel... The person who smiles at me on the street is my angel... Everyone has got my back. EVEN THE FREAKING ANTS ARE MY ANGELS!!!

The eventful day ended with tarot card picking and conscious breathwork. The tarot card that I chose essentially said that I needed to fix my "mommy issues."

At first, I thought, how odd is that... I love my mom and we have a great relationship. And then I remembered that she told me that one time when I was a baby she was walking down the stairs while carrying me and dropped me and I broke my leg.

...What if my "chronic fear" was placed into me ever since I was a baby because of that?

Whether it was or it wasn't, attributing my fear to that put me at ease. My leg healed just fine and I don't consciously remember it. Attributing it to that gave me permission to let go of my fears.

HEALTH IS SO MUCH MORE THAN PHYSICAL HEALTH

When looking at health and wellness, WE CAN'T JUST LOOK AT OUR DIET AND EXERCISE. There is so much more to health! This includes mental, emotional, and spiritual health. You can't just go on a diet or work out more and expect to feel 100% better. It is SO CRUCIAL to identifying the root cause of WHY you don't feel your best and that you're not in your best state of health.

Think about how light you could feel if you didn't just lose weight, but if you released the root cause of what has been really holding you back. This is something that I help new clients with on what I call a "Discovery Phone Call." This is where I ask you questions to help you realize what it is that has been holding you back from being your best self.

This call isn't for everyone. It's for you if you're ready to be committed 100% to your yourself and your goals— which I know that you are if you're making it through this entire book. I hope that you've learned so much that you'll take into committed action, and it helps a ton to verbally integrate everything that you've learned so far which is why I highly recommend going to **adriennerivera.com** now and booking a FREE discovery call with me or someone on my team.

You literally have nothing to lose, just answers that you've been waiting to gain. You may be wondering, why is she doing this for FREE? Because I don't want you to struggle any longer! I don't want you to have another year of failed New Year's Resolutions. I want you to FINALLY SEE YOUR WORTH and take action towards achieving your goals once and for all.

I also know that a certain number of you all are ready to take a leap of faith and will join my 12-week fitness program where we will work together to help you improve your fitness, mental health, stress levels, to get you in the best shape of your life.

And I'm so excited to talk to you, learn more about your goals and get you showing up and going in the right direction every single day of your life! LIFE IS NOW! What have you been waiting for? If you're waiting for a sign, this is your sign!

IT IS ESSENTIAL TO REBOOT AND RESET THE MIND

TOP 10 WAYS TO REDUCE STRESS

1. Mindset Calls - These are important! Even if you think you're good and don't need them, schedule them. We've been creating some powerful breakthroughs for several of you. This is where your resistance is dissolved and you accept that it is amazing to be wherever you're at on this journey. (P.S. - Even if you've already used your call last week, if you need support again this week. Reach out! Please!)

2. Morning "DUMP" Journaling - You all know that I HIGHLY recommend journaling during this process. What I recommend is writing 3 pages every morning of what ever comes onto the page. No prompts, don't make it pretty. Just flush your brain.

3. Prompt Journaling - I've been giving a lot of you customized Journal prompts during our Mindset Calls based on whatever is showing up for you. If you're wanting to explore more prompts, see the following:
- Where in my life is my lack of action actually serving me?
- What have I been resisting or avoiding the most? Where is that stemming from?
- What do I actually LOVE about the parts of my body that I've said negative things to?

4. BREATHWORK - I recommend a style of breathwork where you're breathing in and out in a circular and connected breath for a long duration of time. This style of breathwork serves as the "mirror" for whatever needs to be brought to your attention. We offer group video breathwork sessions as a bonus in our coaching program! There are also shorter breathwork techniques that you can do that you can include into your morning routine.

5. Mantra Mediation - This is where you sit still and focus on a mantra or a phrase, such as "I am breathing in, I am breathing out." I recommend doing this for about 5 minutes.

6. DANCE PARTAYYY - This has been one of my recent favorites! I put on my favorite song of the week and interpretive dance all around my room. It feels so freeing!

7. Chakra Water Cleanse - At the end of your shower, turn the water to cold. Let the cold water cleanse the top of your head fully. Take 3 super slow, deep breaths here as you feel the cold water rinsing away any bad energy that you've acquired throughout the day.

8. Technology Detox Walk - Go outside and walk for anywhere from 5-60 minutes. Leave your phone at home and let your feet determine your route as you go. Observe what's going on around you here as you walk around.

9. ART! - This can be whatever you'd like it to be. You can get a coloring book and crayons, draw in your journal, or experiment with a new art medium!

10. Creating a Night Routine - My night routine starts with "showering/rinsing off the day." Then I turn on my diffuser with essential oils and my favorite candles. I rub my homemade body butter all over my body and pamper myself doing so. It feels amazing! Once the diffuser is on, the day is done! (Also the phone goes on Airplane mode in the furthest corner of the room before I shower)

SHIFT YOUR MINDSET AND STOP MAKING EXCUSES

Have you been making excuses as to why you can't have the results of others because of your limiting mindset beliefs? Our mind creates our reality! Below are some examples on how we can shift certain popular beliefs so that we can uplevel our mindset, own our worth, and live in ABUNDANCE!

EXAMPLE: If working out is hard in your opinion, it will always stay hard...
MINDSET SHIFT: "working out gets to be FUN for me and makes me STRONG"

EXAMPLE: If spending money on your health is an expense, you're not a priority for yourself...

MINDSET SHIFT: "I'm so worthy of feeling the best I can that I LOVE investing in myself."

EXAMPLE: If you are telling yourself that you CAN'T lose weight because you can't give up your favorite foods, the universe will listen to you...

MINDSET SHIFT: "I get to eat an ABUNDANCE of fruits and vegetables that nourish me and give me the energy that I need to be my best self."

EXAMPLE: If you are telling yourself that you "have no time," then you're right. And you're still not prioritizing yourself...

MINDSET SHIFT: "I love myself so much that I'm going to wake up early and get in a 30 minute home workout so that I can feel AMAZING and ENERGIZED the rest of the day."

So, if there's an area of your life that you're trying to change, look at your mindset first and see how you can shift it! Remember that it gets to be easy if you let it be.

START INVESTING IN YOURSELF!

Telling yourself that you "can't afford" to invest in your

health is rooted in a lack of self worth, just like telling yourself that you "don't have time to work out" is rooted in a lack of prioritizing yourself.

It takes GREAT strength to ask for help. Everyone can benefit from it! I have multiple coaches. I invest in myself because I know I'm worthy simply because I exist. I make time to work out because I prioritize my health and happiness—and everyone around me benefits from that positivity. The same could be true for you!

My health & mindset coaching program is SO much more than a fitness plan and nutrition guidance!

- I help you dig deep into negative mindset patterns that have been holding them back.
- I help you release their need to find comfort in food
- I help you learn how to LOVE yourself fully
- I help you release your negative self-talk/comparison to others

As a result, EVERYTHING IN YOUR LIFE WILL BENEFIT!!!

Think about how amazing your relationship could be if you felt SEXY in your own skin... Think about how much energy you could have to keep up with your friends on long HIKES... Think about your new-found CONFIDENCE that will shine through, landing you your dream job or promotion...

I want ALL OF THOSE THINGS FOR YOU!

If you're looking for a sign, this is your sign. This message was put in front of your eyes for a reason Your time is NOW! And I'm here to tell you that you are SO WORTHY OF HAVING IT ALL.

Go to **adriennerivera.com** and schedule a time to talk with us so that you can finally get the results in every area of your life that you deserve!

MEET THE AUTHOR
ADRIENNE RIVERA

Adrienne Rivera is a fitness coach specializing in helping you creating transformational, healthy lifestyles in all areas of life. She believes that long term physical & emotional health can only come from mastering relationships with others, food, fitness, and most importantly oneself.

Adrienne is also a motivation speaker, triathlete, and host of the podcast, "The Fit Through Love Show." She is a National Academy of Sports Medicine Certified Personal Trainer and has a degree in Psychology. She has worked with clients to help them lose up to 50 pounds, helped couples mend their relationships, and assisted many in fixing their relationship with food.

Find her at **adriennerivera.com**, on Instagram at **@fitthroughlove**, or on Facebook as Adrienne Rivera.

To learn more about her about coaching, speaking rates, and retreats send her an email her at **adrienne@adriennerivera.com**!

Made in the USA
San Bernardino,
CA